Archbishop Daniel E. Pilarczyk

'We Believe'

Essentials of Catholic Faith

St. Anthony Messenger Press

CINCINNATI, OHIO

Scripture citations are taken from *The New American Bible With Revised New Testament*, copyright ©1986 by the Confraternity of Christian Doctrine, and are used by permission. All rights reserved.

Cover and book design by Julie Lonneman

ISBN 0-86716-131-0

©1990, Daniel E. Pilarczyk

All rights reserved.
Published by St. Anthony Messenger Press
Printed in the U.S.A.

Contents

Faith: Saying 'We Believe'   1

Creation: The Masterpiece   7

Creation: The Ongoing Story   13

Sin: The Wrench in the Works   19

Incarnation: God's Gift   25

Resurrection: The Fulfillment   31

Incarnation: The God-Man   37

Salvation: The Accomplishment   43

Grace: The Sharing   49

Church: The Community   55

Church: The Mission   61

Trinity: The Source   67

Glory: The Goal   73

Prayer: Addressing the Crazy Lover   79

Faith: Saying 'We Believe'

What does it mean to believe? For one thing, belief means to accept something as true, whether or not we can personally demonstrate its truth. I believe that the planet Mars has polar ice caps and that the Battle of Waterloo took place in 1815. Most information we use in life is composed of this kind of belief. If we relied only on what we could prove or only on what we have personally experienced, we could rely on very little.

We hold certain beliefs about God and religion. We believe that there are three persons in God, that Jesus Christ is both divine and human, that there are seven sacraments. We accept these statements as true, even if we can't prove them scientifically, even if we're not sure of their full meaning.

But believing is something far more profound than merely accepting a statement as true. Believing also means being a believer. It means having faith. Having faith involves accepting truths, but more deeply, having faith means giving ourselves over to a person and becoming part of that person's story, a true story. Religious belief concerns not just a body of truths but a person. Being a believer, having faith, means voluntarily becoming part of the story of God's love for the world, becoming part of the story of the life and destiny of God's Son, Jesus. Faith provides the only scenario that addresses the deepest dimensions of our lives. If we refuse our part in God's story, our lives lose their center and degenerate into meaninglessness.

The story to which we give our lives in faith is a single story. It is based on facts and truths that come together to make a coherent whole stretching from the moment of creation to the last instant of time and on into eternity. It is a love story, a story about God's love for us and about the way God invites us to respond. It is a story in which each of us has an important part, a part that can be played by no one else. It is a story of success and failure, of generosity and sin, of clarity and confusion. It is a story about charity and justice. It is a story that is filled with meaning for each individual human being and for all of us together.

Being a believer, having faith, implies taking God's word, accepting as true God's offer of love and concern for us, living out that acceptance in every aspect of our lives—not just with our minds, important as that is, but also with our hearts and our lives, with our jobs and our friendships, in times of deep reflection and in the humdrum moments that compose most of our life.

Accepting the truths and giving ourselves to the story are both important. A member of the Church is expected to accept what the Church believes and teaches. The believer can recite with honesty and sincerity that compendium of truths which the community prays at the Sunday liturgy and which we call the creed.

But being a Church member is much more than just accepting that list of truths. Being a member of the Church means handing ourselves over to the Lord who stands behind the creed. "Accepting as true" without personal commitment to what the truths imply turns the truths of faith into mere information.

Evelyn Waugh's novel *Brideshead Revisited* has a wonderful passage in which Rex Mottram, a superficial social climber, is taking instructions to become a Catholic so he can marry an heiress. He just wants to know what he has to believe so he can sign on the dotted line. Things go pretty well until the heiress's little sister mischievously tells Rex that Catholics believe that you have to sleep with your feet pointing east so that if you die during the night you can walk to heaven. He's ready to believe that, too, but he wonders why nobody told him before. Poor Rex! He was ready to sign on to a list of "truths" but not to engage himself in real faith. He was ready to "believe" but not to be a believer.

On the other hand, committing ourselves to a faith which does not have clear and specific teachings is an exercise in emotionalism. Accepting the truths of the creed constitutes the bones and muscles of faith; committing ourselves to what the truths mean are the soul and spirit of faith.

Handing ourselves over to God to play our part in God's love story for our world and our life is not necessarily easy. Often society neither welcomes religious belief nor regards it as important. Gestures appear at Christmas and Easter, but mostly our culture tells us that real importance lies in scientific knowledge and technology, success and wealth, prominence and power here and now, looking out for oneself, avoiding pain and providing for ourselves the maximum amount of comfort and pleasure. Not all of these things are bad, of course, but in God's love story they are all secondary themes. They are not the main plot. Yet society insists that faith is the secondary theme, that religious belief is a nice thing for those who find it helpful but that reality is elsewhere.

Being a believer is hard because so many voices on the stage where God's story is being played out keep saying that it is basically irrelevant. During the last 18 months a 20-story office building has been going up next door to the church complex where I live. Now the church building is overshadowed by the still-unfinished office building. Those two buildings symbolize faith and the world. What used to be a highly visible church now seems insignificant, as if the world were trying to cut faith in God down to size.

Still other factors contribute to making belief difficult, factors within ourselves. Sometimes our life seems so heavy, so confused, so meaningless, so sinful that we find ourselves wondering how God can really love us. Sometimes we wonder if the truths that underpin our commitment to the Lord are real. Did God create the world? Is Jesus divine? Is the Church actually part of God's story? Does an eternity of happiness await us?

More often than not such questioning and confusion offer an opportunity for growth in our faith life. After all, faith does not placidly accept a body of statements which remain obvious and clear forever. Religious faith is not a geometry theorem or a cold historical fact. Religious faith is, rather, a personal relationship, a love affair between ourselves and the Lord, a love affair between ourselves and those the Lord loves. Every personal relationship implies growth. We change as our lives progress. Things once important seem less so at another time. Things once clear cloud over as our circumstances change.

As our relationship with God deepens and develops we face challenges within ourselves, challenges to our selfishness and superficiality. Just when we think we have figured out our part in the story, we find aspects that don't seem to fit in. New approaches and new emphases are called for. This can be devastating if it leads us to give up our part in God's love story. But growth and maturity will come if we hold on to our relationship with the Lord and weather the storm in the company of Jesus and his Church. The struggle to understand and to accept is part of the life of faith, part of being a believer.

This book offers neither an exhaustive account of Catholic belief nor a list of truths which we are expected to accept if we would be Catholics. Its purpose is to outline the story in which we are all invited to take part, a story about creation and sin, about Jesus and the Church, about grace and glory, about God and about us. The story is composed of truths—not truths for their own sakes but, rather, as foundations for faith, for our participation in God's story. To take seriously our part in the love story that God has written for our life and for our world is the commitment we make when we say, "We believe."

For Discussion

1) What is the difference between "accepting truths" and "giving yourself over to God's story"? Why are both important?

2) What factors in our society today make it difficult to be a believer?

3) When have questions or confusion about your faith led to personal growth?

4) In what ways does your faith challenge you?

Creation: The Masterpiece

"Marley was dead to begin with.... This must be distinctly understood, or nothing wonderful can come of the story I am going to relate." These words which begin Charles Dickens's "A Christmas Carol" are appropriate as we begin to reflect on the love story between God and the world, between God and us human creatures, a story in which each of us has a part. You have to know the beginning if you want to understand the story.

God's love story begins with time itself, a beginning recounted in the first chapter of Genesis: "In the beginning, when God created the heavens and the earth..." (Genesis 1:1). The account goes on to tell how God created light and the sky and the earth, vegetation, the stars, the animals. Finally God creates human beings, male and female, giving them charge over all the earth. Then "God looked at everything he had made, and he found it very good" (Genesis 1:31).

This beginning of God's love story has two main points: (1) The world was created by God and (2) it was good.

Creation (and this includes the whole universe, not just the planet earth) did not happen by chance. Creation was not a casual coming together of cosmic gasses but a purposeful project undertaken by an infinite intelligence. Whether God at the beginning created everything exactly as we know it today (which seems unlikely) or whether God created a process which evolve in time according to God's purpose is a se question. The main point is that our universe and our world are the result of God's will—an intelligent will, a free will, a will acting with a purpose, the will of the all-powerful and all-loving God.

The Genesis account makes clear God's role as creator, but it also tells us that world which God created was and is good. In the history of human thought, some have looked on the world as fundamentally bad, the product of the powers of evil, to be tolerated at best, sometimes to be rejected. Even today some can see nothing of the world's beauty, nothing of its wonder—only pain, confusion and despair. Such an attitude is simply not in accord with the truth we believe.

At the same time, this good world is not God. Sometimes people are so entranced with the beauty and the power and the variety of creation that they see no need to look for anything beyond it, and so make the world into God. This is not correct either. Although the world reflects the goodness, richness and creativity of God, the world is distinct from God, different from God and not nearly good enough to be God.

What we have in the world, then, is God's will at work, a work freely undertaken which is distinct and different from God, yet not opposed to God or separated from God.

Among the creatures inhabiting God's good world, the most important is the human being. Genesis tells us that God made the human creature to reflect its Creator differently than others: "God created man in his image;/in the divine image he created him;/male and female he created them" (Genesis 1:27). Here we see the human part in the story that God was beginning to write, a part greater than that of other creatures. A human is not just one more animal.

We also see that human beings are essentially communal, and act to be solitary. Men and women were created to work

What does all this say to us, millions or billions of years after God created the heavens and the earth?

For one thing, it tells us to celebrate creation, to enjoy it. Although the world is not our final goal, neither are we confined here as a punishment. It is the product of the loving will of a loving God who has left traces of love everywhere to remind us of our origin and our destiny.

The world has problems, of course. We shall see more about that later. Sometimes the problems seem so great that the term *world* is used, in Scripture and elsewhere, as a synonym for everything opposing God. But the basic truth remains that the world is good because it was made good by the good God, who was beginning a love story that would go on forever.

Those who examine the world, rejoicing in its complexity and beauty, help us grasp these truths more firmly. Take the scientists, for example. Some research the smallest building blocks of created reality while others look towards a seemingly endless series of stars. Some catalogue the thousands of species of animals and plants which have never been described before. In the human body actions and reactions are just now being discovered, while others remain for future generations to learn about and wonder at. There seems to be no end of natural phenomena that God has placed in the world, partly to keep its unimaginable complexity in balance and partly, perhaps, simply to express joy in the act of creating. We can almost imagine God saying, "Let's make a few more species of animals! Let's create another galaxy or two! It's good! It's very good!"

Artists describe the beauty of creation so that the rest of us can enjoy and appreciate it even more. They have been given the gift to see and make others see what might otherwise be taken for granted: the splendor of a wildflower, the brilliance of a bowl of fruit, the depth of meaning in a human face, the majesty of a human figure. We speak of artists as creative. More exactly, they reflect the creative genius of the good God who has created a good world, a world so good that much of its beauty would never be appreciated if it were not called to our attention.

Some artists work in words. They describe the complexities of human relationships. They point out to us the tragedies and the comedies of human existence. Every great novel somehow comments on the creation of humankind in the image of God, and every great poem comments on what God saw when first looking on creation.

Teachers spend their lives helping others to know and remember what past generations have learned about the world, what past generations have done in the world. In the last analysis every teacher reflects the worth and the goodness of creation.

But God's creative power and the goodness of the world say still more to us. They tell us that the world is not a plaything with which to amuse ourselves and then cast aside. The world resulted from God's creative love and reminds us of that creative love. It is meant to be taken seriously. For that reason we are called to respect creation. Creation is ours to use, but it remains God's. This truth has a particular urgency at a time when we have discovered ways to make the world uninhabitable through our abuses of water and air and food, not to mention our apparent capacity to destroy it completely with the weapons we have contrived.

Respect for God's creatures has a special meaning in our dealings with other men and women. Every single human being is made in the image and likeness of God. Every single human being is unique. For those reasons there is a certain inviolability, a certain sacredness about other human beings which the rest of us are called to defend and foster. We are not free to kill other human beings, to mistreat them or to allow them to live in inhuman misery or to despise them because of their race or nationality. Every human being has a privileged place in creation and, as participants in the world, we are all called to defend that privileged place. We are called to love other human beings because we are called to love God, who loves everything that has been created.

The world in which we live comes from a loving God. The world in which we live is fundamentally and perennially good. We must grasp these foundational truths if we are going to understand and accept the part which God calls us to play in the love story that is the story of the world. In the beginning, when God created the heavens and the earth, the stage was set on which that story was to be played out. It is a good setting for a good story.

For Discussion

1) What truths about creation do you find in the opening chapters of Genesis?

2) Why is evolution an interesting but only secondary question about the meaning of creation?

3) What connections do you see between the meaning of creation and contemporary concerns about ecology?

4) What connections do you see between the meaning of creation and the attitude that we should have toward other human beings?

Creation: The Ongoing Story

God didn't create the world a long time ago and then walk away. God did not set the stage and then leave the theater. Creation is still going on today.

Creation's ongoing existence indicates that God's creative love continues to operate. The world subsists not out of its own power, but out of God's love. If God tired of it or somehow became distracted and forgot about it, even for an instant, all creation would simply cease to be. The world around us is a sign that God is still saying, "Let there be light and sky and earth and vegetation and animals and human beings." The world continues because God's creative action continues.

We know that the world developed in stages. Geologists describe periods when most of the world's surface was covered with ice. Species of animals have come and gone. Dinosaurs are no longer with us, and today's horses and cows are of relatively recent origin. The world's climate has changed many times. Some formerly temperate parts of the world are now almost uninhabitable, and vice versa. All sorts of things have happened since the beginning. All sorts of things continue to happen. God's power is still at work. God has not yet finished with creation.

But God's ongoing creative work is perhaps most obvious in the world's chief creature, humankind. When God gave the first human creatures dominion over the world and told them to cultivate it, God invited humankind to participate in the development of the world. God called men and women not just to use the world but to collaborate in making it, to be its cocreators. God created and still continues to create a world that has a history, primarily a human history.

Several important implications are inherent in God's creating a dynamic world. One is that human beings have a responsibility not just to respect and reverence what God has created, but also to develop it, to use it in a way that takes advantage of all the wonders God has put in it and brings about new wonders. When we speak of human creativity we are speaking about the gift of ingenuity which enables us to play our part in carrying forward God's creativity.

In carrying out this responsibility, human ingenuity discovered fire, iron, then steel; how to build wheeled vehicles moved by animals, then wheeled vehicles which move themselves, then vehicles that move through the sky. While exploring and enhancing the possibilities of creation, human ingenuity found a way to fly to the moon, only the beginning of exploring space.

But human participation in God's creativity is not limited to what we can do with inanimate elements. Human creativity also deals with the development of humanity itself. As the centuries passed, humankind learned how to speak, how to share our deepest feelings with one another. We developed various patterns of living together: in wandering tribes, in villages and cities, and now in an increasingly common, global society. We have come to know and care for our bodies more effectively so that we are healthier and more long-lived than our ancestors. We have taught ourselves to think with increasing complexity, so that we can now deal not just with the pursuit of the next meal, but with the structure of the universe and even, in some way, with the very nature of God.

As we consider human participation in God's ongoing creation of the world, we should recall that responsibility for the world belongs to each and every one of us. We all have our parts to play. Some—heads of nations, great thinkers, distinguished scientists—seem to have lead roles, while the rest of us spend less time in the limelight. But in fact, we all depend on each other. If statesmen, philosophers and scientists worked all alone, nothing would happen.

Some—perhaps most—important happenings in creation are never in the limelight at all: parents' care for their children, the love of a married couple, the affection friends share, the charity of a saint. A little reflection on our individual histories reminds us of the effect that people have on one another. What we are today is due in large part to how other men and women have affected our lives.

We do not always see how our life fits with other people's. We do not always realize the effect that we have on others. The ongoing process of human development is often too complex for that, both at the individual level and at the level of human history in general. But the reality is there. Simply because we are human beings, we are each and all called to share responsibility for God's world, particularly for the world of humanity. We are each and all called to participate in God's creative activity.

In all of this we must remind ourselves that God, too, has an ongoing part to play in creation. God is not over there watching disinterestedly as we do our thing. On the contrary, God is working in and through us. God has created the life of each of us. God has a destiny in mind for each of us. God is interested in each of us. As we attempt to carry out our role in the world, God stands by us, nudging us now in one direction, now in another, inspiring us to do this or that, leading us to carry out the divine plan for us and for those around us and, indeed, for the whole of creation. We are all responsible agents in the development of creation, but we are also all instruments of the all-wise and all-loving God.

We call God's action in the lives of each of us "divine providence." If it were not for divine providence, our responsibility for creation would be a crushing burden instead of a glorious adventure.

Sometimes even people of faith find it hard to see divine providence at work in their lives. "How can my life make any difference?" we ask. "How can God bring anything out of what I am doing here and now?" "How can my suffering do anybody any good?" We find ourselves asking questions like these because we tend to underestimate God's goodness and God's power. We think God is about the same size as ourselves and works as we do. In fact, God is infinitely more than we are, and the God who created the whole universe out of nothing is the same God who promises to be at work in our life.

The fundamental truth here is that we are all important, important to God and important to the story of God's world. Each human life has something to contribute to the ongoing process of creation. If we lose sight of this we run the risk of falling into meaninglessness. We begin to think that we are insignificant, a grain of sand in a galaxy. We become paralyzed, because if we are insignificant and without any real meaning, there is no reason for us to strive, no reason for us to extend ourselves, no reason for us to do anything. Our lives become what Thoreau called "lives of quiet desperation."

Many people in our world struggle along this way. In fact, there was a whole school of philosophy which dealt with human existence in terms of *ennui*, boredom. One member of that school, Albert Camus, said that the only basic question of human life is the question of suicide.

What God offers us is much more than boredom and the

possibility of suicide. God offers us a glorious world, a world filled with beauty, a world so complex that we will probably never exhaust its mysteries. Even more, God offers us a part to play in that world. God calls us to share in its creation, to help make it what it was destined to become from the beginning. Nobody else can play the part that God has written for each of us. Our part in the drama may gain little notice from the other participants in it, but we believe that it is a part that is eternally important to God. Otherwise we wouldn't be here.

For Discussion

1) What are human beings called to do beyond having respect and reverence for God's creation?

2) What things in your life are of tremendous value yet not "in the limelight"?

3) Are you aware of God's presence and activity in your life?

4) In what sense is everyone a very important person? Why is it very important to believe this?

Sin: The Wrench in the Works

God's creation is good. God's plan for the development of creation is good. By rights, then, we should be living in a world in which the creative love of God is gratefully accepted and everybody is working together to bring the world to its ultimate fulfillment. The human story should be a story of collaboration and accomplishment in what God intended for creation from the beginning.

But it's not. If we simply look around us we realize that something has gone wrong. We see people filled with hate. The most intimate human relationships turn sour with self-serving and rejection. People seem driven to possess the world's goods in endless quantity, far beyond what is needful. Joyful collaboration with creation's Lord is lost in a blind pursuit of immediate satisfaction. The good of some becomes an occasion of gnawing envy for others. God's gifts are received as if by right and used as if their human possessors were in total charge of them. Humanity's basic relationship with God is turned into a burden or even into a matter of radical indifference.

Disarray in God's creation is not limited to individuals. In social systems whole groups of people are despised and deprived of their rights because of their race; in economic systems people live and die in misery; in political systems service to others is replaced by the domination of the weak by those who are most powerful.

Something is wrong here, and that something is sin. There are many ways to define sin: unhealthy pride, an inflated sense of our own importance, the deliberate violation of God's law or rebellion against God's plan. Another way to think of sin is as irresponsibility, an unwillingness to play our part in God's plan of creation. In sin, the main character in God's story for the world, the human character, decides that the script offered by God isn't good enough and begins to ad-lib.

We are all infected with sin. Maybe our sins are not major acts of outrage, but they are in our lives nonetheless: acts of unkindness, great or small, to those around us, excessive use of food and drink, petty selfishness that keeps us from sharing with others what we have and what they need, indifference to our relationship with God expressed in thoughtless prayer, irregular worship or even in a total disregard of God. A common expression of sin is the inclination to believe that we have no sin, that our lives are basically without blame, that our sinful choices are not really bad at all—or, even worse, that there is no such thing as sin.

Our sins are personal, but they are also social. Because we are gifted with free will, we share responsibility for the world. We may not be accountable for the origins of our society's injustice and oppression and lack of care, but we are accountable if we allow these sinful situations to continue. Sin is not just individual personal behavior; it also exists in the systems for which we are responsible.

Sin is personal, social and pervasive. In act or in consequence it is everywhere. There is no untainted island to which we can flee to be free of contact with sin. Sin is not outside of us. Sin is rooted deeply in every human heart. We cannot flee from it because we cannot flee from ourselves.

But why do we sin? What makes us incline to irresponsibility toward God's creation and toward our part in it?

Why does wrong so often seem so right?

For one thing, we have an inborn tendency to fall short of our destiny. Somehow we find ourselves instinctively selfish, instinctively irresponsible, instinctively lazy. We are born morally defective. God didn't make us that way. God did not short-circuit the plans so carefully made for creation. God doesn't undermine the divine plans. We Catholic Christians believe that this inborn inclination to sin is the result of a human decision which somehow broke off the original loving relationship between humankind and God. Like everything else in creation, sin had a beginning. That beginning left its imprint on everything that followed. We are born with an inclination to sin because we belong to a species which inclined itself to sin. That first decision, that beginning of the human sinfulness which we all share, we call "original sin."

To understand original sin properly, some things need to be clear. Original sin in us is not a sinful act for which we are responsible and for which we will be punished. Original sin is not something that we committed before our birth. Nor does God punish one person for the sins of another. Rather, original sin is a congenital, spiritual deficiency within us, a weakening of our ability to relate with God. Original sin, as applied to us, is a condition and not an action.

The Church's teaching about original sin is not exclusively bad news, however. If we did not know about original sin, it would be impossible for us to understand how or why so much sinfulness exists in the world. Likewise, if we did not know about original sin, we would have to conclude that each of us is born morally perfect, with full potential to live a sinless life and that, if we do not live up to that potential, the blame is ours alone. Given who and what we are, we are simply unable to live totally sinless lives or to expect a totally sinless world. Knowing about original sin makes us realistic about ourselves.

Original sin, that first turning away from responsibility in God's plan, is not the only reason why we sin. We also are *taught* to sin. From our earliest moments we are in touch with people who are sinners. We unconsciously absorb sinful attitudes about love and hate, about wealth, about ambition, about self-sufficiency. No one sets out to make us bad, but we cannot help absorbing something from the world around us as we become aware of it. We consciously experience people who do wrong but are apparently successful and happy. Over and over again, we notice how attractive the short-term satisfaction of sin seems. Over and over again, we are shown ways to get around our responsibilities as agents and instruments of God's plan for creation. It is not that everybody around us is trying to enlist us in a conspiracy of sinfulness; rather, sin is so pervasive that we cannot help being influenced by it.

We also sin as a result of our own past sins. Every time we go off on our own way, every time we shirk our responsibility as God's agents in the world, sin becomes easier the next time. Sin has deep roots, and once the plant begins to grow it is not easy to get rid of.

Two more things should be noted about sin: First, pervasive and infective as it is, sin remains a secondary element in God's good world. The world remains what God made it: a reflection of God's own goodness and beauty. It is still basically good, despite all the misuse humankind has inflicted on it. Consequently, as we consider the sinfulness of the world, the appropriate response is not despair but hope.

Second, God has not abandoned the world. Despite that first rejection of God's plan, a rejection that still affects each of us, and despite the contribution that each of us makes to the undoing of God's story line for creation, God is with us still. In fact, God is with us in ways that seem to surpass the original plan. Even taking sin into account, the story continues to unfold, and in many ways it is a better story than before, as we shall see.

With sin humankind threw a monkey wrench into God's works. But God is loving and powerful enough to keep the works going in spite of the wrench, indeed to make them work better.

For Discussion

1) Give examples to illustrate that sin is found not just in individuals but also in social, economic and political structures.

2) Why are people inclined to think of themselves as having no sin or even to deny that there is such a thing as sin?

3) What evidence have you seen that sin is rooted deeply in every human being?

4) Why is the appropriate Christian response to sin not despair but hope?

Incarnation: God's Gift

God's response to human irresponsibility was not to turn away. God did not leave us to our own devices. Instead of abandoning us to our own sinfulness, God sent us Jesus as a gift to sinful humanity. Jesus did not appear as some strange visitor from outer space to sort everything out for us in spite of ourselves. Rather, Jesus was a human being who lived a human life in the midst of human beings, in the midst of human history. Therein lies the real significance of Jesus' life. To downplay the humanity of Jesus runs the risk of making him incomprehensible.

Jesus was born and grew up in backwater towns. He spent his life in an obscure country. He took part in the religious life of his people and his time. He was not a world figure while he lived. In many ways he seemed pretty ordinary. He learned, as we do, a little bit at a time. He experienced fear and anger and disappointment and failure. He was tempted, as we are, to turn aside from his human responsibility toward God.

Jesus' work during his time in the world was that of a religious teacher. To all who would listen he spoke about God's love for us and about our love for God. He taught that God loves us abundantly, more than we can imagine. He taught that God loves us all, sinners though we are, Jews and non-Jews alike. Jesus opposed the idea that God is merely a lawgiver and that our duty is to observe God's law in order to claim God's attention. God is much more than that. We are much more than that. Jesus taught his followers to look on God as an extravagantly loving parent. He himself called God *Abba*, "Father" or "Daddy," and found peace and renewed energy in the long periods of time he spent in prayer.

Jesus had harsh words for those religious leaders who claimed worth on the basis of their own presumed righteousness rather than on the basis of God's generosity, those who were ever ready to accuse others of sinfulness and religious impurity. He had no time at all for hypocrisy and was eloquent in his criticism of those who would make a relationship with God into a burden.

The center of Jesus' teaching was the Kingdom of God. He spoke of a whole new relationship between God and humankind in which sin would be destroyed, in which all pain and suffering would be transformed, in which God's blessings would be shared by everybody, in which people would enjoy unbelievable intimacy with God. Jesus taught that the Kingdom had already begun in him as he worked miracles, giving sight to the blind and hearing to the deaf, even raising dead people back to life. Jesus also offered forgiveness to sinners. All this was to serve as a sign that something wonderful and new was at hand, that God's creation was entering a new phase.

Another important aspect of Jesus' life and teaching was his friends. He loved people, all sorts of people: women, children, men. His closest followers were those we call his apostles. They were not intellectual giants or socially important people but a group which included some small-time fish merchants, an internal revenue agent, and one or two who might be suspected of political radicalism. They were ordinary men, not particularly bright and, as it turned out, not particularly courageous. But Jesus loved them and enjoyed being in their company.

Jesus was friendly with other people, too—people who were not nice. He seemed to have a special fondness for spending time with men and women who were rejects in the religious society of his time: people who made no secret of their sinfulness, men and women who were free and easy about the observance of religious ritual, those who collaborated with the Roman overlords and so had put themselves beyond the pale of acceptability. Nobody was too bad or too outrageous for Jesus to notice and love. This was a real scandal to those who exercised religious leadership. How could Jesus claim to be a teacher to his people if he kept giving attention to men and women like that?

In what Jesus taught and did people found new hope and new freedom. If God's love is as abundant as Jesus said, if every human creature, even the least important, has a special dignity, if all are called to participate in the Kingdom of God which has already begun, then Jesus was presenting a whole new world. People no longer needed to be ashamed of themselves, to feel the oppression of not really belonging or the despair of not knowing where to turn in their sinfulness. True, there was still sin in the world, there were still injustices to be dealt with, there was still the hypocrisy of the self-righteous to be healed, but the Kingdom that Jesus preached put all this into a new perspective. What he was proclaiming and practicing was nothing less than a revolution—not the revolution of the terrorist or the political opportunist, but a revolution of one who spoke for God, a revolution which would reorient the whole of creation.

That's why they killed him. The life and teaching of Jesus seemed so radical, so dangerous to the religious and civil authorities that they arranged to have him executed on false charges. Jesus was put to death as a criminal.

The death of Jesus was not just an injustice, not just the brutal termination of one more human life. The death of Jesus was a real act of witness. He was put to death precisely because of what he had taught and done. He was a martyr to his own life-style, to his own teaching. If he had been willing to compromise, to tone down what he was saying, to tell the people that they had misunderstood him, he might have saved himself from death on the cross. After all, the attack on him from the leaders of the people did not come as a surprise. Jesus saw it coming for a long time. Yet he remained faithful to his calling, faithful to his teaching mission, faithful to what he knew God expected from his human life.

Jesus was a human being who lived a human life like ours, a life that began with birth, that evolved through a certain number of years, and that ended with death. That fact is essential to the meaning of his story.

But from another perspective, Jesus' human life was quite different from ours. To a greater or lesser extent we live in selfishness and sin. We often try to turn creation in a direction other than God's. We overlook our responsibility to develop humanity into what God meant it to be, and instead settle for immediate personal satisfaction. When we look at our world, all too often we don't see the handiwork of a loving God in which we are called to collaborate, but a collection of opportunities for us to exploit. When we look at God, all too often we see not the infinitely loving God Jesus called Father, but the stern Lawgiver or the irrelevant Architect. When we look at our brothers and sisters in humanity, all too often we see not creatures of priceless dignity, but tiresome men and women who make our life uninteresting and difficult.

Jesus' life was different. Yet its significance does not lie so much in his sinlessness—although that is an important aspect of it—but rather in the fact that Jesus' life was what God had meant human life to be from the beginning. Here at last was one who understood the glory and love of God, a glory and a love reflected in creation yet reaching far beyond the visible world. Here at last was one who collaborated in God's plan for the world by bringing men and women to appreciate their dignity, by calling them to love one another, by teaching them the worth of even the most insignificant of their brothers and sisters, by making them aware of the depth and intensity of God's love for them. The priorities, categories, goals and values that Jesus exemplified in his life are those that God intended all human beings to live by when we were first created.

To say that Jesus lived a human life is absolutely correct and theologically precise. But in view of the significance of that life in the story of ongoing creation and in the story of God's human creatures, we could also say that Jesus lived not just *a* human life but *the* human life, the human life par excellence.

But all this is only the beginning. Other facets of the reality of Jesus are still more wonderful, still more significant. His life and his mission did not end with the cross. In a way, as we shall see in the following chapters, they only began there.

For Discussion

1) Explain how the Kingdom of God was the center of Jesus' teaching.

2) What was so radical about Jesus that led to his being killed?

3) Why is it important to understand that Jesus was fully a human being, like us in all things but sin?

4) What implications does Jesus' association with the "rejects" of his society have for a Christian today?

Resurrection: The Fulfillment

If Jesus' life had ended on the cross, his story might have been a high point in creation. Here was someone who had apparently done everything right, had followed out God's plan for the world in his words and actions, had attempted to contribute to the development of what God had begun in the human creature, had apparently demonstrated how rich and how spiritually profound a human life could be. It was an exemplary life.

But if Jesus' life had ended on the cross, his story would also have been one of the saddest stories in the history of creation. He who carried out God's will as none had done before would have died leaving behind only a memory of rejection and failure, done to death by the fear and narrowness of his fellow human creatures. If Jesus' life had ended on the cross, his story would be just one more monument to the triumph of human irresponsibility, to the triumph of human blindness, to the triumph of sin. Everything would be the same as it was before, with Jesus as the great exception proving the rule of futility in human endeavor.

But Jesus' life did not end on the cross. Soon after he had died he reappeared. He came back to his friends and followers. They recognized him as being the same Jesus they had known before, even though he was somehow different. His greeting to them was a greeting of peace. He calmed their fears at seeing him by assuring them that he was not a ghost. On many different occasions he joined them again when they were gathered to recall his memory, when they sat together at meals, even when they worked at their fishing business.

He continued to teach them. He explained to them how his life was the fulfillment of everything that God had planned for creation and humankind. He told them that they would soon receive his Holy Spirit, and that they were to forgive sins even as he had. He pardoned them for their cowardice when they had run away from him, and said that he would be with them forever. Most important of all, Jesus told them that they were to carry his teaching about the Kingdom of God throughout the whole world without fear, that his life was not to be an end but the beginning of something which would last until the end of the world.

After a time the disciples did not experience him in the same way any more. But they knew that he was still active in their midst because he had promised that he would be and because they found in themselves courage and power and enthusiasm that had not been there before.

The significance of the Resurrection of Jesus lies in what God says in and through it. In bringing Jesus gloriously back from death God is saying that a life like the life of Jesus is too good to end, too important to be overcome by human sinfulness, too significant to be relegated to the realm of mere memory, too precious to be the freak exception in the story of creation.

By raising the humanity of Jesus from the dead, God is giving a sign of divine approval to Jesus' life. God is saying, in effect, "The life of this man is what human existence is all about—love and friendship and compassion and faithfulness and self-sacrifice, total dedication to the divine plan for creation, total giving of the human self to the work of the Creator even if the short-term result is rejection and death. This is what I want human existence to be and I want it to be so gloriously and forever." The Resurrection is God's "Bravo!" for Jesus' part in the story of creation. Finally somebody had done it right! Jesus had played his part exactly as written by the Author and the Author wants it never to end. That's why the humanity and the life of Jesus did not come to a close with his death. It is still going on. It is still important to God. It is important for us.

To understand the Resurrection of Jesus appropriately, we must realize, first of all, that Jesus' Resurrection was a radical transformation. Jesus' followers knew that it was he whom they were seeing because they had known him so closely during his life. He still carried the marks of the nails in his hands and feet. He ate with them after the Resurrection as he had done before. He remembered them, who they were and what they had done. They were able to give witness that it was the same Jesus.

But Jesus was different, also. He walked through closed doors. He came and went at will and appeared in unexpected ways. Even though he was the same Jesus, his friends did not always recognize him right away. He was the same Jesus, but he was not a revived corpse, come back from the dead to start living again in the same old way. He had been changed, transformed, glorified—still human but translated to a whole new level of being.

We have to be quite clear about Jesus' bodily Resurrection. His body rose from the dead, the same body that it had been before. The theological sophisticates who are indifferent to whether or not Jesus' body decayed in the tomb are missing one of the most important aspects of the Resurrection. The identity of the glorified Jesus after the Resurrection with the historical Jesus who had been put to death on the cross is supremely important because of what it says not just about Jesus and his life but also about God's good creation and about God's plans for that creation.

The bodily Resurrection of Jesus is a revelation about

human life. Transforming Jesus and raising him from the dead is God's message about an unsuspected potential in created reality. In Jesus' new life, a life untrammeled by the constraints of space and time, we become aware that not all that exists is destined for decay. We come to understand that this world and God's plans for it hold more than what we see. We learn that human life is not destined for death and failure, but for transformation and glory—not in some metaphorical way, as we might speak of a glorious memory, but really and truly. In the Resurrection of Jesus the second act of creation begins, an act as real as the first and even more exciting.

The Resurrection of Jesus, however, is a reality that can be perceived only by faith. Sometimes we find ourselves wondering how Jesus got out of the tomb. We wonder whether the soldiers tried to stop him as they saw him walking away. We wonder why Jesus didn't go to Annas and Caiphas and Pilate and rebuke them for their cruel injustice to him. But all of that is irrelevant to what the Resurrection is really about.

The Resurrection of Jesus is not just one more event in the history of the world, not just one more set of circumstances subject to human inquiry. The Resurrection of Jesus is *beyond* human history. No eyewitnesses saw Jesus step out of the tomb because the Resurrection was an act of God that carried Jesus beyond the ordinary human categories of time and space into a whole new realm of being. The only way to be in touch with the Resurrection of Jesus is to be in touch with the realm of God through faith, to have handed ourselves over to God's realities, to have offered ourselves to play our part in God's story—a story in which the Resurrection of Jesus is a major climax. That doesn't make the Resurrection any less real. It simply means that we cannot deal with it in the same way we deal with the material realities around us.

And yet the resurrected Jesus has witnesses. Those who have come in touch through faith with the reality of the risen Christ in their own lives, those who have accepted the full reality of God's love as manifested in the life of Jesus are witnesses to his Resurrection. The faith of each of us is a testimony to the power and reality of the risen Christ. *We* are the witnesses to the life and power of Jesus, who is with us today as he was with the apostles on the first Easter.

Finally, we need to observe that the Resurrection of Jesus was not just something nice that God did for one man at one point in time. In fact, the Resurrection of Jesus is of fundamental and intimate importance to all creation, to each of us now. We shall explore that more fully as we reflect more on the reality of Jesus in our next chapter and on the implications of the Resurrection in the chapters which follow.

For Discussion

1) What do you think the significance of Jesus' life would have been had it ended on the cross?

2) What do you think God is saying to us through the Resurrection?

3) Why is the Resurrection a reality that can be perceived only through faith?

4) What does it mean to say that we today are the witnesses of the power and reality of the risen Christ?

Incarnation: The God-Man

Soon after Jesus rose and returned in his risen and glorified body to his Father, the Spirit came upon the apostles. These weak and cowardly men were changed into enthusiastic witnesses to the Kingdom that Jesus had preached. But there was more to the coming of the Holy Spirit than an infusion of courage. The apostles not only began to behave differently; they also began to see things differently.

As the apostles reflected on the two or three brief and eventful years that they had spent in Jesus' company, they realized with increasing intensity that Jesus had been more than he seemed. They reflected on his miracles, on his forgiveness of people's sins, on his teaching that a person's final value would be judged by what that person had done to Jesus. They reflected on the special meaning that he seemed to give to the phrase he liked to use in describing himself: "the Son of Man." He was often called "Lord," a word used to address God. Sometimes he allowed himself to be called "Son of God" and to be referred to as "the Christ," the promised savior.

Jesus' relationship with God seemed different from other people's. He seemed more familiar with God, more in tune with God. Jesus referred to God as *Abba* ("Daddy"), which seemed to indicate that he enjoyed a relationship with God that others did not. Then came the Resurrection and glorification of Jesus. Was it merely a sign of approval from God for what Jesus had done and said during his public life, or was it a sign of something more?

As the apostles and the other followers of Jesus reflected on him under the guidance of the Holy Spirit, they became aware that Jesus was indeed more than he seemed. Jesus, full and complete human being, was at the same time no one less than God.

Jesus' followers gathered together the story of his life, death and resurrection. They began to express, as best they could, the astounding truth of which they had become aware: Jesus was God who had lived in their midst. Soon these accounts were written down by those who had heard the apostles and ultimately became the Gospels in the New Testament.

Then there was Paul. Paul may have known about Jesus and his earthly life, but he certainly didn't understand what Jesus was or what his life was all about until his experience on the road to Damascus (see Acts 9:1-6). After that Paul took his place with the other apostles. Paul's letters to various Christian groups form a large part of the New Testament. In these letters Paul speaks of Jesus as one who, although divine, did not cling to his equality with God but emptied himself to assume the condition of a slave (see Philippians 2:6-11) and as "the image of the invisible God," who existed before anything was created and who holds all things in unity (see Colossians 1:15-20).

By the time the last parts of the New Testament were written, the divinity of Jesus had become ever clearer, so that the Gospel according to John says, "In the beginning was the Word.../and the Word was God..../And the Word became flesh/and made his dwelling among us..." (John 1:1, 14).

The whole New Testament is a series of writings about Jesus, who lived and died a fully human life, but a life through which he revealed himself to his followers as one truly divine. That was the message the apostles were sent to deliver; that is the message that has come to us.

But if Jesus was God, why didn't he just say so? Why didn't he come right out and tell the apostles so they could tell everybody else? Basically because it would have been too much for them to take. They knew God as totally other, unapproachable, awesome. Until they had experienced the full force of Jesus' life and teaching, they would have been overwhelmed with fear or incomprehension or even outrage at the very idea that anything human could also be God. They needed to experience the warmth of Jesus' life, the power of his teaching, the tragedy of his death and the glory of his Resurrection as well as strengthening from his Spirit before they could even begin to understand.

Even then they could only speak in halting words, because there wasn't even a vocabulary to express what they had experienced. Believers would struggle for centuries to find a way to understand and to speak precisely about what it meant for Jesus to be both God and man.

Some said the human in Jesus was merely an appearance. Others said that Jesus' divinity was only God taking a human being to himself and making him a son by adoption. Still others said that the human and the divine were united in Jesus because the divinity of God took the place of the human soul of Jesus. The Arians contended that Jesus was *almost* God, a kind of semidivinity who had charge of the world but, in the last analysis, was only a creature. The Nestorians taught that in Jesus existed two subjects—two entities, two persons—one human and one divine, who worked in harmony and that the person of God dwelt in the human person of Jesus as in a kind of temple. Still another group, the Monophysites, thought that humanity and divinity were mixed together in Jesus in such a way that his humanity was really absorbed by his divinity.

These attempts to understand and express the reality of Jesus all failed because they didn't adequately account Jesus as really God, or because they didn't adequately account Jesus as really human, or because they separated divinity and humanity to the point that Jesus was not one being but two.

Conclusive theological formulation of the reality of Jesus came at the Council of Chalcedon, more than 400 years after the apostles. The Church solemnly defined that Jesus was (and is), in one and the same subject, perfect in divinity and perfect in humanity, and that his divinity and his humanity are united without mixture, without change, without division, without separation.

If we still do not grasp the fullness of Christ or the total significance of his story, at least we have a terminology for thinking about him and about the realities which must be preserved as we deal with Christ in faith.

Dividing up Christ is not something confined to Church history books. Some people today refuse to believe that Jesus was divine. For them, he may be a great teacher or a splendid model of human behavior, but that's all. Others refuse to accept that Jesus was human. They think of his life as effortless, without the real pain and frustration that every human experiences. Both approaches are wrong; both are incomplete because neither accounts for the full reality of Christ.

If the Christ we reverence is not fully divine, if the Christ we worship is not fully human, if his humanity and his divinity are not united in a single subject, then the Christ we are dealing with is not the Christ of the apostles or the Christ of the Christian faith, but a figment of our own imagination.

But what difference does it make? Granted that Jesus was a real human being, what does it add to say that he was God? Granted that he was God, why bother about whether he was really human? The Christian answer is crucial when it comes to considering our own relationship to God in redemption and grace and glory, when it comes to considering the community of believers which is the Church, when it comes to figuring out what our human existence ultimately means.

To say that Jesus is one being, both human and divine, is to say that in him God became a human actor on the stage of the world's history, that God became a human participant in the love story that had begun with creation. With God as a human participant, the story takes a whole new turn, and so does our part in it.

For Discussion

1) What types of memories did the disciples reflect upon in coming to terms with who Jesus is?

2) During his earthly life why did Jesus not preach more about his own identity and his relationship with the Father?

3) Why do you think it took several centuries for Christians to formulate basic terms and concepts for understanding Jesus?

4) Express in your own words what it means today to say that Jesus is one being, both human and divine.

Salvation:
The Accomplishment

We have spoken about creation: God's good creation and God's plan for our collaboration in creation. We have spoken about sin, about the way in which we human creatures have misused and continue to misuse what God has given us, about how we have acted and continue to act irresponsibly in regard to what God has invited us to do in creation. We have spoken about Jesus, about his life and death, about how his life was the perfect human life, lived as God had meant all human life to be lived and how, therefore, Jesus was raised from the dead in glory as a sign of God's approval of his life. We have also spoken about Jesus as God, the Son of his Father, fully human yet fully divine. Now it is time to talk about what Christ accomplished through his human existence.

As the God-man, Jesus was not just one more human being. His life was not just one historic episode in God's creation. Jesus' human life was, of course, the human life par excellence, but if that's all it was, we would have been worse off than we were before—still struggling with our sins, but now looking with despair at the example of him who had done things right in a way beyond our imitation.

As the God-man, Jesus lives more than human life. God is present to every time and place; therefore the human life of Jesus, united to God without separation, becomes present to every time and place. Through the power of his divinity, human life is transformed. The divine and human life of Jesus offers humankind a whole new way of being. Just as in Jesus God became human like us and took a human part in the story of creation, so also the life, death and resurrection of Jesus, divine and human, both invite and enable us to become like him—not just in his humanity but in his divinity as well. He makes his divine life available and accessible to us, so that we live our human existence transformed by the power of his divine Spirit.

God was so taken with Jesus' life that he wanted every human creature to live the life of Jesus. When Jesus comes into our lives, God recreates us, reshaping our human qualities through the love of Jesus. Our human life becomes Jesus' life, human and divine.

This is *salvation*. This is what it means to say, "Jesus has saved us." In ordinary terms, saving is the opposite of throwing away. The criterion for saving or throwing away is worth or value. We save what is worth something to us; we throw away what is not. Saying that we are saved by Christ means that God makes us worth bothering about. Salvation makes us precious to God in an entirely new way because it makes us like Christ, both human and divine.

In addition to speaking of what Christ accomplished in his life as "salvation," the Christian tradition also speaks of it as "redemption." *Redemption* means being freed, being liberated from a situation of imprisonment or confinement. When we are redeemed by Christ, we are transported into a new context of freedom.

Because we become like God, we enjoy freedom from sin. In our purely human existence everything seems to go wrong, everything seems somehow to be mixed up with evil. When we are redeemed we are assured that we need not be overcome by sin. The powers of sinfulness within us and around us will not have the last word because the life we live is no longer just a human life but the life of Christ, a life whose ending is not defeat but transformation.

Redemption also frees us from death. This does not mean that our earthly life will go on forever, but that our earthly death is only a stage on the road which leads to the full manifestation of what God has made us to be. For those who are redeemed, suffering and death, real as they are, are not the final realities but a prelude to something far different and far better. Our life, like Christ's, is directed not toward death but toward resurrection.

Redemption also frees us from the law of achievement. In this world of ours, nothing is free. We each have to make our own way, and those who cannot are driven to the wall. But the life of Christ which comes to us with redemption is not something we earn. We cannot earn it because we cannot make ourselves worthy of something so far above us. We receive it as a gift of God or we receive it not at all. Once we live Christ's life, all merely human striving fades into relative insignificance. Even a life that seems to end in failure, like Jesus', is a life destined for glory, like Jesus'.

Once we share in Jesus' life, everything changes. We no longer need to suffer alienation or loneliness, to be enslaved by fear or despair or meaninglessness. Things that turn life into hell on earth for so many people can now be surpassed, transcended, transformed by the life of Christ that goes on in our life. Likewise our human accomplishments, those few things we can be proud of—our acts of concern for others, our love for family and friends, our understanding and improvement of the world around us—all these are transformed and elevated because they are not just our accomplishments but also the accomplishments of Christ, who lives in us.

The life of Jesus, then, is not over. It goes on in his risen humanity, in us. Through his divine humanity, the life of Jesus has come into our life. We no longer live alone. We live with and in him.

What is true of us individually is also true of the world as a whole. Thanks to the life, death and resurrection of Jesus, divine and human, our world is no longer merely the creation of God, good as that is. It is now the place where God's human and divine activity in Jesus continues to unfold. It is God's world in a way in which it was not before God became a human participant in it. It has been given a new direction and a new significance.

All this is what we mean when we say that Jesus saved and redeemed us.

Now perhaps we can see how fitting it was that Jesus was both human and divine. If Jesus has been merely a human being, his life would have been, at best, an example. On the other hand, if God had chosen to restore the world without the collaboration of humanity, the restoration of the world would have been an acknowledgement that things had gotten so bad that they could only be dealt with through an interruption from outside. By redeeming and saving the world through humanity, the humanity of Jesus, God indicates that the original plan was a good plan. God acknowledges our inherent worth by using one of us to save and redeem humanity from ultimate failure. We have been saved and redeemed through the power of God, but we have also been saved and redeemed by a human being like ourselves. God has an ingenious way of doing things.

The life, death and resurrection of Jesus, therefore, were not just a flash in the pan, an intermezzo in an ongoing history of the misuse and mismanagement of God's good world. On the contrary, the saving and redeeming event that was Jesus' life was a whole new beginning for the world and its human creatures. It constituted the beginning of the second act of the story of creation. And the second act will end quite differently from the first.

Many questions remain. How are we transformed by the salvation and redemption which Christ accomplished? What does it mean in practice for us to live the life of Christ? If Christ lives in us, how and why do we still sin? If the world is God's in a new way, thanks to the presence and activity of the risen Christ, why is it still such a sorry place? These are urgent questions, and their answers lie in what the Christian tradition calls grace.

For Discussion

1) What do you think it means to say "Jesus has saved us"?

2) From what do you sense salvation in Jesus has set us free?

3) In what ways might you consider God's plan of salvation "ingenious"?

4) What difference has the life of Jesus made in your own life?

Grace: The Sharing

In the Christian tradition, grace signifies Christ's life in us. In ordinary speech *grace* means "charm" or "appeal" ("a very graceful person"), but the word's root meaning has overtones of kindness, favor and gift. In Christian belief, therefore, *grace* suggests God's goodness and generosity, which endow us with the life of Christ. Grace is gift par excellence.

Grace is our sharing in the salvation and redemption of humankind that was accomplished by the life, death and resurrection of the God-man Jesus. It is a new kind of relationship with God. When we are in the state or relationship of grace we, as individuals, have been created again so that the life of Christ continues and evolves in our individual human existence. In a way that only God can bring about, we live Christ's life in our own.

It important to realize that grace is a gift, freely given us by the Spirit of God. We cannot earn or deserve this relationship because we can have absolutely no right to it. Left to ourselves, we would remain in constitutional, personal sinfulness, muddling through as best we can, looking to God as something outside ourselves. But God does not leave us to ourselves. God comes to us on God's own initiative and makes us over so that, in addition to being ourselves, we are also somehow participants in the life of Christ. Yet we do have a part to play in grace. God does not make us sharers and participants in the life of Christ whether we want to be or not. God *offers* us the new life of Christ as a gift which we may accept.

Moreover, grace is not just an individual matter between God and ourselves. Grace is offered to us through other human beings, through and in the community of those who believe in Christ which we call the Church.

All this comes together and is expressed in Baptism. (Most often we think of Baptism as something for babies. In fact, Baptism is primarily for adults. The Baptism of infants is conferred in view of an adult relationship with God which exists in the Church and in the child's sponsors and family and which will develop as the child assimilates personally what he or she is given at Baptism.)

Presenting oneself for Baptism expresses a willingness to share in the life of Christ, to be part of God's story for the world in and with Christ. The candidate expresses faith. (Note that even this preliminary faith is itself the gift of God and not something achieved for ourselves.) Through the ministry of the Church in Baptism, God transforms this incipient openness to Christ and establishes a new relationship between the candidate and Christ. God gifts the candidate with Christ's life. The candidate is precious to God in a whole new way. The candidate now shares not only the life of Christ, but also the lives of all others who live in Christ. We come into grace, then, and into the Church, through God's gift in faith and Baptism.

What does this mean in practice? First of all, from God's perspective, the newly baptized person is no longer living merely as creature but someone living and continuing the human life par excellence, the life of Christ.

From our perspective, grace in practice is a matter of priorities. If we consciously and conscientiously live the life of Christ, our scale of values will be different from that of people who have not accepted Christ. Money, for example, will mean something different to us. So will success. So will friendship and marriage and work and leisure. So will sickness and death. All these things and others have a different meaning to those who live in Christ simply because Christ's life is a different life.

Moreover, living in grace precludes serious and deliberate sinning. The New Testament teaches clearly that we cannot live Christ's life and at the same time be murderers, thieves or slanderers. We cannot live the life of Christ and indulge ourselves in sexual irresponsibility or jealousy or quarreling. It is not that the relationship of grace makes us incapable of sinning, nor that God becomes angry with us when we sin and calls off the relationship between Christ and us. Rather, by such conduct we make it impossible for Christ to live in us and, as it were, drive him out of our lives. Sinful behavior is incompatible with the life of grace; where sin exists the grace of Christ cannot be. This is easy to understand if we remember that another way to speak of grace is as holiness, the holiness of Christ.

If all this is true, how and why do people who are supposed to be believers, who are supposed to be living the life of Christ, behave the way they do? For that matter, why do we ourselves behave the way we do sometimes? Our priorities are not always Christ's. We all sin. If our life is the life of Christ, how can this be?

Grace does not overwhelm us and make us do what we are supposed to do whether we like it or not. On the contrary, just as we must exercise our human freedom to *accept* the life of Christ in faith, so also we must exercise our human freedom to *assimilate* his life and carry it out in our lives. God respects our freedom. God invites us to recommit ourselves to faith and to Christ over and over again, day by day, in a thousand human decisions and choices, big and small. Grace, the life of Christ, develops in the life of the individual. We can respond and grow ever stronger in Christ; we can neglect grace and grow indifferent; we can even reject it completely. The decision to accept our part in Christ's story is only the first of many, and it needs to be reaffirmed in every circumstance of our lives—not because God is ungenerous, but because our human collaboration and response are important to God. Human freedom is an essential factor in Christ's ongoing life in grace just as it was in the earthly life of Jesus.

This also explains why the world is still so clogged with sin, selfishness and irresponsibility. Society and culture, the contexts in which we live, result from human decisions. Human decisions have made the world the way it is and human decisions keep the world as it is. If, after the life of Christ has been unfolding on earth for 20 centuries, the world is still a mess, it is not because the life of Christ has been ineffective but because it has been so effectively rejected by generations of human beings (even Christian believers). Just as God does not force individuals to live out Christ's life consistently as individuals, so also God respects human freedom in the social and cultural context. The story of the world is the story of Christ's life, but it is also the story of human freedom.

A few more observations about grace need to be made if we are to avoid misunderstanding. First, grace is a spiritual gift, not a psychological experience. We don't necessarily perceive or feel it. Feeling good about God no more proves the presence of grace than questioning or struggle indicates its absence.

Next, grace is more than God treating us *as if* we were like Christ. Grace is a real interior transformation that makes us infinitely different than we were before.

Finally, grace is not a bus ticket to heaven, an object which God gives us and which we have to hang on to if we want to be saved. Grace is the life and holiness of Christ given to us by the Holy Spirit. It calls for response and development from us. We are called to live out the life of Christ, not merely to possess it.

Grace, then, is participation in the salvation and redemption accomplished by Christ. Grace is the story of the life of Christ extended to all ages and all places. Grace is also our story, our part in his life, played out in our time and in our world in the company of all those who believe in him. And that brings us to our consideration of the Church.

For Discussion

1) How is a good grasp of grace helpful for understanding Baptism?

2) Why is Baptism only the beginning of our new life in Christ?

3) With grace so readily available, why is there still sin in the world and in your own life?

4) How has your own experience of grace influenced your attitudes and values?

Church: The Community

Grace is the life of Christ, extended by the Holy Spirit into the lives of individual believers. Because there is only one Christ, all who accept Christ participate in one life. All of us together constitute one Christ, and being in Christ through grace means being together with all others who are in Christ. This community of believers in Christ, established and held together by grace, is the Church.

Our common life in Christ is a spiritual reality. We can't see grace or test for it as for radon. Nonetheless, the community of believers which is the Church is more than a spiritual gathering. Just as Jesus' humanity was visible and palpable, so also his Church is a visible organization, involved in the story of creation and redemption with its own earthly reality, its own history and its own particular activity. Because the Church exists to carry out and continue the life of Christ, the activity of the Church reflects and expresses the activity of Christ.

The Church is primarily both sign and agent of grace, bringing Christ's holiness to its members. This is the meaning of its sacraments. In Baptism, the "constitutional" sacrament, the Church acts as sign and agent of God in conferring the life of Christ on believers. Baptism both symbolizes and brings about the life of grace in the baptized person; at the same time, it makes the person a member of the community of those who share that life.

The other sacraments deepen and make explicit the life of Christ at various moments in the life of the believer or consecrate the believer's life for particular service in the community. Thus Confirmation offers strength for living out the life of Christ in our human existence. The Eucharist nourishes us in the life of Christ. When we sin, the Sacrament of Reconciliation offers us forgiveness and renewed life in Christ. When we are seriously ill, the Sacrament of Anointing offers us courage to face our suffering in union with the life and suffering of Christ. Matrimony confers the holiness of Christ on the human relationship of love between woman and man. Holy Orders establishes the deacon, priest or bishop in a position of special service to the life of Christ in the Church.

All the sacraments are actions of the Church. All the sacraments are the actions of Christ. All the sacraments are signs and instruments of the grace of Christ in the life of the believer.

As minister of holiness the Church also prays. In the liturgy, its corporate and formal worship, the whole community of believers offers praise and thanksgiving to God. There we all pray and Christ prays with us and in us. The worship we offer to God in the Church is not just ours but his as well. It sanctifies us because it is done with and in Christ.

As Christ taught, so also the Church teaches. It presents and perpetuates the teaching of Christ. It reflects on the teaching of Christ and his apostles in order to understand their implications and applications for us today. Just as the sacraments are not the action of the Church alone but of Christ as well, so also the teaching of the Church is not just the thought of human believers which we are free to accept or reject, but the teaching of Christ himself. The Church teaches with the authority of Christ because it is Christ who teaches in the Church.

As Christ was a leader, so also the Church leads. It provides direction for its members just as Christ did for his apostles. It calls them to express the holiness of Christ's life in their own lives. It provides the laws and rules which are necessary in the life of any human community. It presents common modes of expression for prayer and faith. Some in the Church are entrusted with a special call to leadership: the Church's ordained ministers who, in different ways and to different degrees, are charged with expressing the Church's teaching and guiding its worship. They are servants of the other members, called to help them live the life of Christ.

But the Church is also a community composed of human beings, with all that implies. For one thing, there is sin in the Church. Its members are all still assimilating Christ's life; they are not perfect. That's why each church building has confessionals or reconciliation rooms, monuments to the sinfulness of the faithful. We all suffer because of the sinfulness and limitations of the Church's members, including its leaders.

This imperfection does not indicate that the Church is not the extension of Christ's life, but only that those who live the life of Christ in the Church have not yet fully and finally made it their own. (This is why sinners, even serious sinners, are not automatically expelled from the Church. They may have rejected the life of Christ through their sins, and to that extent are members of the Church in an irregular and lifeless fashion. But they maintain a relationship with the Church because the life of Christ once existed in them through grace and can be renewed if and when they repent.)

Likewise, the Church is not the Kingdom of God, that final state when all things are fully enveloped in the love of God through Christ. In the Church we have the beginnings of the Kingdom. The Church directs us toward the Kingdom through its teaching and sanctifying activity as well as through our life together in the community. But the Church here and now is not the Kingdom pure and simple.

For all that, the Church is not optional, not something just for those who like organized religion while others go it alone. To share the life of Christ and deliberately reject the Church is not possible, because to reject the Church is to reject the life of Christ.

This is not to say that all those who are not officially Church members are automatically out of touch with the life of Christ. There are degrees of contact with the Church and therefore degrees of membership in it. Not only baptized Catholics share the life of Christ which is grace. Some Christians, for example, reverence God's word in Scripture and celebrate Baptism but not the other sacraments. Others accept almost the whole of the teaching of Christ and the Church, but not the Church's visible leadership (the pope and the bishops). Some people have never even heard of Christ or have never had Christ adequately presented to them, but strive to live their lives in reverence and responsibility. To all of these Christ in some fashion offers a share in his life.

Yet *full* incorporation into the Church means living the life of grace, worshiping God with Christ in the liturgy and the sacraments, accepting Church teaching and recognizing Church authority. Christ calls all humankind to this degree of full membership.

The life of the Church, then, is the life of Christ, visible and active despite human faults and deficiencies. This community holds together in the holiness of Jesus' life, expressing and fostering that life in, through and for its members.

When Catholics reflect on the Church, they reflect also on Mary, the Mother of Jesus. This is not just because Mary had an essential role to play in the birth and life of Jesus or because we revere her for her sinlessness or because we rely on her intercession for us with Christ in heaven. All that is true, but there is more: Mary's part in the redemption and her continued association with Christ exemplify the Church itself. Virgin and mother, Mary conceived Jesus through the intervention of the Holy Spirit and gave him to the world. So also the Church brings Christ into being in the faithful and offers him to the world not through its own human power, but through the power of the Holy Spirit. At the end of her life Mary was assumed into heaven and now lives in glory with Christ—the state for which we believe the Church is destined.

Mary has been called the model of the Church. If we want to see the nature and the mission and the destiny of the Church expressed and carried out in the life of just one member, we look to her. We turn to Mary to find out who and what we are as Church.

For Discussion

1) In what ways is the Church an extension of the life of Christ? In what ways is the Church distinct from Christ?

2) Each of the seven sacraments is unique but, at the same time, all in common are "signs and instruments of grace." How have you experienced Christ's action in the sacraments?

3) What does it mean to you to say that Mary is a model of the Church?

4) How does the community of believers make a difference in your own life?

Church: The Mission

The Church shares Christ's life in space and time as the community of those living in grace. But the Church is more than a spiritual club or a warm and friendly place where we feel secure in our common participation in the life of Christ. God gave the Church a mission to address not just its own members but the world at large, a mission in which all the Church's members are called to join.

The Church's mission is to reshape creation into the image of Christ. Once God became human in Jesus, creation had a new goal, a new purpose: to reflect God as manifested in Jesus. The story of creation became the story of Christ. The love and reverence for God and humankind that Jesus taught and exemplified are to be manifested in every aspect of the world, in every human activity, in every human endeavor. This mission is carried out by Church members—all of them—living and acting in the world.

The Church is primarily an organization of laypeople. Priests and bishops are not the "real" believers and other members of the Church mere objects of their pastoral care. Neither does the value of a layperson's life depend on how much the person does for the Church community. Laypeople are baptized and confirmed believers whose primary responsibilities lie outside church sanctuaries. They live and work in the world. The Church exists to bring the life and the love of Christ into the world. Therefore laypeople bear prime responsibility for carrying out the Church's mission in the world.

Consequently, one of the Church's primary responsibilities is to enable laypeople to carry out their responsibilities *as laypeople* in the world. Church ministers, whether clerics or laypersons who work in the Church, serve the general body of the Church's members; they enliven and assist them in carrying out the Church's mission of witness and action in the world.

Church members carry out this mission by acting in the person of Christ in their particular segment of the world. They are called to do as Christ did: namely, to make holy, to teach, to lead. Church members make holy their segment of the world by showing the holiness of Christ and by inviting others to share that holiness. They teach by expressing in their lives the teaching of Christ and by living out its implications. In doing these things, Church members lead the world toward its final destiny, complete life in Christ.

In practice, carrying out the Church's mission is not a matter of pious posturing or preaching. Fulfilling the Church's mission requires extending personal concern to those around us, changing situations offensive to human dignity, conscientiously and generously contributing to the destiny of creation and being motivated not by greed or ambition, but by something—Someone—beyond the sphere of ordinary human activity. The believer in the world asks the question, "If Christ had his way here, how would things be?" The answer to that question provides the agenda for the believer's life and work, an agenda which often enough involves effort, sacrifice and misunderstanding. Carrying out the Church's mission in the world is much more than just "being religious."

What is the scope of the Church's mission? Every context in which humans are involved calls for the presence of Christ and therefore for the witness and work of the Christian believer. Probably no complete list exists, but the basic human relationships are obviously included: family, friendships, marriage and the relationships we form in the course of our job or profession. Christ wishes to be present in all of these.

Also included are the more complex relationships that form the society in which we live: neighborhood, local and national government, unions, the courts. The way our country is run and, indeed, the way the world is run depend on human attitudes and human decisions and are therefore open to the influence of Christ working through those who believe in him.

Then there is culture, that complex of attitudes and practices which provide the day-to-day atmosphere in which we live. Our culture pays lip service to human worth and human dignity but abuses humanity by abortion, pornography, tolerating poverty and canonizing wealth and power. Such a culture does not adequately reflect the love and the life of Christ. The Christian believer has work to do here.

We live in still other contexts: sports and entertainment, the media, the academic world, science and medicine, industry. In fact, little goes on in the world which is not somehow affected by humankind, and all of it calls for life in Christ.

All of these human contexts need the influence of Christ's life and love to be in final accord with God's love story for the world. They need to be remade in Christ's image—and that will happen not through some miraculous intervention from on high but through lay Christian believers who conscientiously carry out the mission of Christ's Church in the world.

God wants to be in charge of the world through Christ. The world's destiny is the Kingdom of God, a full and acknowledged lordship exercised by Christ Jesus. The mission of the Church is to work for the coming of that Kingdom. This mission is exercised in every context in which a Christian believer lives out the implications of the life and teaching of Christ.

The reality of the Church, both as community and in its mission to the world, is most eloquently expressed in the celebration of the Eucharist. At the celebration of Mass, the Christian community comes together under the leadership of its priest and in the company of Christ. We are instructed by God's word in Scripture and the homily. We offer God the gift of our lives—all our actions, our thoughts, our words, our work, our relationships—symbolized by the bread and wine presented from the congregation.

Working through the priest, the power of Christ transforms these gifts into his own Body and Blood. In the process we relive with Christ the supreme moment of his earthly existence: his definitive offering of himself to the Father in his death on the cross. But now it is not his offering alone, but ours as well. When we receive Communion, we receive the Body and Blood of Christ, his life, to nourish our life in him. In the Eucharist, then, we are taught and sanctified. Our lives are given over again to Christ. We are strengthened in him.

But the Eucharist is not just a refuge, a chance to get away from our struggles and our problems in the world and spend some time together with Christ. The life of Christ in us is a life to be shared with the world around us. Every celebration of the Eucharist ends with an agenda for us. The agenda is God's will for the world, God's plan that the reality of Christ be brought into factory and store, neighborhood and office, friendship and family. We are not free to decline the agenda because it is an integral part of the Church's life, an integral part of our lives as believers, an integral part of the Eucharist.

The Eucharist is the heart of the Church. It is an action of praise and love and thanksgiving to God on the part of the Church, united with Christ. Its power impels us to bring to our world the energy and the life of Christ. Everything the Church is and does is somehow directed toward the Eucharist. Everything the Church is and does somehow has its source in the Eucharist. We understand the Church and the Church's mission to the extent that we understand the Eucharist.

For Discussion

1) In your own words describe the mission of the Church.

2) Why is it important to think of the Church as an organization primarily of laypeople?

3) Name some concrete ways that Church members carry out their mission in the world.

4) In what ways do you carry out the mission of the Church in your own life?

Trinity: The Source

As the story of creation, incarnation, redemption and Church unfolded in the context of human experience, another dynamic was also at work. A deeper theme gradually became clearer as Jesus' disciples reflected on their experience of Jesus' life, death and resurrection, as they set out to live and share and proclaim the life of Jesus in the Church. This theme speaks not only of God's love for the human creature but also of the intimate, interior life of God before and beyond creation.

God has made us in the divine image, loved us in spite of our sinfulness, entered human history in Jesus, recreated us in Christ's image and brought us together as Church. In all those actions, God has also quietly and gently been telling us about what and who God is, about the power, sharing and love that were before the beginning, that are the source and form of everything, that are the goal to which everything is directed. Through our experience of creation and Jesus and Church, God allows us to touch and to know the very divine center. God has revealed to us the mystery of the Trinity.

The triune God was part of the apostles' experience with Jesus and was at the center of their preaching. But only after several centuries of reflection did the Church evolve theological formulation about the Trinity. This formulation can be summarized in a few words: God is one; and in God are one divine nature and three divine Persons, Father, Son and Holy Spirit. Son proceeds from Father, and Spirit from Father and Son.

What we are dealing with here is mystery. It is important to be clear about what we mean by *mystery* in a context like the Trinity. Mystery is not a problem to be solved, least of all a mathematical problem about how three can be one. Mystery is an inexhaustibly knowable truth, a reality beyond full comprehension, an expression of something which is understandable in part but whose full significance is beyond human intelligence and human words.

What, then, does the experience of the apostles and the Church enable us to understand about God?

Jesus spoke of God as Father, but in a way suggesting a deeper and more intense relationship than anyone had experienced or expressed before. God as Father meant something different to Jesus than it does to us. As the apostles (with the help of the Holy Spirit) reflected on their experience of Jesus, they came to understand that Jesus himself was nothing less than God. Jesus was not a copy of God, but himself God, fully human but also fully divine, fully known by God and fully knowing God.

Jesus promised to send the Holy Spirit upon the apostles. The Spirit came on Pentecost and enlivened them with a love and an energy never experienced before. The Spirit Jesus sent was not a ghost, not a metaphor like the "spirit of Christmas past." The Spirit Jesus sent was nothing less than the love that is shared between Father and Son, a love of divine proportions, distinct from Father and Son yet God as they are.

The Church's experience of Jesus teaches us that in God is community, that God is source, that God is knowledge, that God is love. God is not some cold philosophical reality, existing quietly and all alone; rather, God is one who knows and loves. In God is Father, ultimate origin and power; in God is Son, the Father's full self-knowledge known and expressed so fully that the Son has a personhood of his own; in God is Spirit, a love between Father and Son so intense that it expresses itself as distinct from Father and Son, yet one with them in being God. We speak of God as a Holy Trinity, a Holy "Threeness," three Persons yet one God.

As we reflect on what Jesus and the Church have expressed in speaking of this innermost life of God, we associate creation with the Father, redemption with the Son, and the ongoing, loving life of Jesus in the Church with the Holy Spirit. We cannot deal appropriately with any of these episodes in the history of God's love for us unless we deal with them in the context of the Trinity, because the Trinity is the source and pattern of everything in the story of God's relationship with creation. The triune God is behind it all, a God who has wanted us to know who and what God is.

But two other matters are still unresolved. The first question is this: Why didn't God just come out and tell us about the Trinity? Why were we left, as it were, to figure things out for ourselves on the basis of what Jesus said and did?

For the same reason that Jesus didn't just tell the apostles that he was God: the reality would have been so overwhelming as to be meaningless. The whole pattern of revelation before God became human taught that God is one. Before anything else God had insisted that the Old Testament people learn that there are not many gods but one; that the realm of divinity is not a world of many competing powers but one unique, almighty Power; that the realm of divinity is not exhausted in the forces of creation but is something far beyond what we can see or imagine, much less portray in images.

Then, with Jesus, God made us ready for more. Through the power of Jesus' life, death and resurrection and through the enlightenment of the Holy Spirit, we became capable of entering more deeply into knowledge of the personal life of God. God didn't just tell us because we learn best when we are shown rather than told. So God *showed* us about the Trinity through Jesus.

That still leaves the second question: *Why* did God reveal the intimate life of the three divine Persons to us? Why did Father, Son and Holy Spirit want us to know about their being, their relationship?

The answer is infinitely profound and yet infinitely simple: because God loves us.

When human beings love each other, they want to share themselves. They communicate. A mother tells her children stories about her youth, about how she met their father, about how things were in the early years of their marriage. She doesn't merely want to communicate information. She wants to communicate *herself* because she loves them and wants to share all she is with them. An engaged couple does the same thing. They talk about their likes and dislikes, about their families, about what has happened to them since the last time they were together. They communicate continuously because they are in love, and being in love means sharing yourself.

Of course, complete communication between two human beings is impossible. None of us can really tell everything about ourselves because we don't really know everything about ourselves. Yet we continue to try in words and actions because sharing ourselves is the center of loving, and the attempt to share continues as long as love lasts.

That's why God has shared the mystery of the Trinity with us: simply because God loves us. We can understand some of what God has shown us in revelation. Much, perhaps most, lies far beyond our powers of comprehension. In spite of that, God strives to share the truth of the divine inmost being with us because loving means sharing and God loves us.

But there is still more. God's communication with us is not limited to sharing information. God also intends us to share the very life and intimacy that is shared by Father, Son and Holy Spirit. That's what we mean by glory.

For Discussion

1) How would you explain the doctrine of the Trinity to a non-Christian friend?

2) What does it mean to say that the Trinity has been revealed yet still remains a "mystery"?

3) God wants to communicate with us about what and who God is because God loves us. How does that compare to your experience of love?

4) In your own prayer life, to which person of the Trinity do you most often turn? Why?

Glory: The Goal

The Father remakes us into the image of Christ through the action of the Holy Spirit so that we can live as Christ lives—not just here and now, in this mortal life, but in the future beyond time that we call eternity.

Jesus in heaven is both human and divine. He participates in the interior life of the Trinity that belonged to the Son before all ages. He also retains his humanity, glorified after his death and resurrection. Because we share the full life of Christ, we too, when our earthly life is over, will retain our humanity, glorified through our association with the risen Christ, but somehow we will also share in his divinity. We will be who we are, but we will also be who he is, all that he is. Just as the Son became human to be like us, in the final scene of God's love story, we will have an eternal and glorious share in being God like him.

The words we use to describe the final goal that God has in store for us—words like *heaven*, *glory*, *eternal happiness*—are bland, perhaps because we use them so casually. Their real meaning is difficult to imagine. We may conjure up images of angels and harps, but deep inside ourselves we wonder whether a changeless eternity might not be just a bit boring. Therefore let's examine more closely God's ultimate plan for us.

To begin, God's plan surpasses all human understanding. It is mystery. God loves us so much that even he does not—perhaps cannot—fully express to us how things will be when we reach our final goal.

But glory does imply continuance of what we know and experience in our life now. We will somehow retain our individuality and our body, but be released from the constraints of the physical world and liberated from the body's capacity for suffering, just as Christ is.

Glory also implies fulfillment. The potential that God created for each of us will not be lost, but will be actualized and brought to term in the glorious humanity of Christ. Our capacity for loving and being loved, for intellectual achievement, for appreciating God's works and for communicating with others, the things we might have been but never got the chance to be, the things we started but never got the chance to finish—all will be brought to completion in the life of Father, Son and Holy Spirit manifested in us.

Likewise, the good that we have done and the blessings that we have received will still be ours. Recollect the finest moments this life offers: the love of family and friends spoken and shared, the few really generous and disinterested actions we have performed, the sense of accomplishment at finishing a long and difficult project, the exhilaration we sometimes experience through music or poetry, the sense of awe and gratitude that occasionally comes in prayer or liturgical celebration, all the moments of special intensity that we wish could last forever. All that will be ours in eternity, affirmed and enhanced beyond our wildest imagination in a glowing instant that will never end, validated by the love of Christ, transformed in the life of the Trinity.

Eternal glory, then, is a matter of intensity, of fullness of life. We do ourselves a disservice if we choose to think of it in terms of an endless succession of what we experience here and now.

Yet the glory of heaven is not just something "out there." It has already begun "in here." Our life now provides, as it were, the base material from which our eternal happiness will be formed. We don't sit back and wait for heaven while passing the time in meaningless human activity. We prepare ourselves for the glory of heaven by our thoughts, words and actions now. Heaven already has its roots in us. Eternal glory is the flowering of what God has already planted in us and called on us to cultivate.

This explains the Christian view of death. Christian believers look on death not as an end, but as a change, as one moment in a succession of moments. Death is simply the final, definitive sum of our life. At that instant, what we are is transformed to glory to the extent that what we have become in our lives is capable of being associated with Father, Son and Spirit in their life forever. Because nothing impure or tainted can be taken into the life of God, the marginal defects remaining when our earthly life ends are somehow purged or corrected by God's action. That which is not capable of life in God—our sins, our selfishness, our rejections of God's love in the course of our human existence—is rejected.

We speak of this as judgment—but we do not mean judgment as a legal process in which God weighs evidence and then announces a sentence. Rather, this judgment is the final revelation of what we really are when all pretense has been stripped away and all our hiding places closed to us, when we ourselves come to know our real goodness without earthly ambiguity.

If heaven's eternal glory is the flowering of God's action and our response and if judgment is the manifestation of our relationship with God at death, then hell is simply the state of those who have no relationship with God to be transformed into glory. Hell is not a *place* in which God puts people who have not found favor. Hell is the *situation* of those who have deliberately closed themselves to participating in heaven by rejecting God's love. To be in hell is to have made oneself an eternal outsider. We don't like to think about hell but, if God has given us the freedom to accept and collaborate with the gifts we have been given, then God has also given us the freedom to reject those gifts entirely. God didn't create hell to keep us in line. Hell is merely the flip side of human liberty.

Each human life, then, is a process of getting ready for glory, of getting accustomed to being with Christ so that we are capable of enjoying his presence forever, of developing God's gifts in our life in such a way that they will fit into the life of the Trinity when our earthly life is over.

Heaven's glory, however, is more than relationships between God and individuals. It is a corporate affair. Heaven is an eternal sharing in the life of Christ and, as we have seen before, sharing in the life of Christ is something we do not alone but as part of the community of all who share his life. In the state of glory we will not only be happy in the company of those we have personally known and loved during our lifetime, but we will also rejoice in the companionship of all those who have shared the life of Christ, consciously or unconsciously, from the beginning of the world to its final instant. The glory of each will be the glory of all. Heaven will be the ultimate Church, the Church first modeled by Mary, the Mother of God, the community of all those who have accepted Christ transformed into the community of the blessed.

The glory of heaven is the goal for which God did everything that has been done in the story of the world, in the story of salvation. The world was created, humankind came to be and to act in the world, God became a human being who lived and died and rose from the dead, salvation was offered to sinners in and through Christ's Church—all for the sake of God's glory, for the sake of our glory. From before the beginning God wanted us somehow to be part of the total happiness of Father, Son and Spirit. Into that happiness God has already begun to gather those whose earthly lives have come to an end. When the world's history reaches its conclusion, God will gather all together in love. The Trinity is at the beginning of all that is, of all that happens. The Trinity, Father, Son and Spirit, also stands at the end of it all, calling all of us to share in the glory of God.

For Discussion

1) How does what we call "heaven" have its roots in this life?

2) How would you explain these concepts: judgment, purgatory, hell?

3) What things in this life give you hints about what heaven might be like?

4) What would heaven be like if you could design it yourself?

Prayer:
Addressing the Crazy Lover

What, then, does belief mean? In the final analysis, faith means accepting our part in a story, in God's story for us. This complex story is carefully plotted. Each element is related to the other parts; no part can be tampered with or overlooked without risk of making the whole story incomprehensible. Reaching from before the dawn of creation to beyond the end of time, this is a story about God's generosity and patience, about human blindness, about Jesus and about his Church, that awesome community of saints and sinners which continues the life of Jesus everywhere and forever. The story unfolds over the background of God's own life as Father, Son and Holy Spirit and ends in glory with all the actors celebrating their parts in it in the company of the Author.

God's story is our own. Our whole purpose is to contribute to and develop the story. Every human life has meaning because every human being has a part to play in God's story. Sometimes our part does not seem very big. We wonder whether our contribution is really important. But God is a skilled author and even the smallest bit player provides something that no one else can. If we had no part, if our existence really didn't make any difference, God would not have called us out of nothingness onto the stage of life, for God does nothing without purpose.

But why did God do it? Why did God bother with this world? Why did God construct such an elaborate stage with so many characters and such extravagant surprises in the course of the plot? Why did God invite us to be part of such a glorious finale? The answer takes us to the very core of belief, to the very foundation of faith. Yet the answer is so simple that even a child can understand it: God did it because God loves us.

Nothing explains that. God didn't and doesn't need us. The Trinity of Father, Son and Holy Spirit have the fullness of all being and life in themselves. Nobody can add anything to the divine happiness. Yet God created the world—and what a world! And God stuck with the world. In spite of human irresponsibility and sin, God continued to be interested; so interested, in fact, that in Jesus God actually came into the world to play a saving part in its story, a part which opened whole new vistas of life for all who would accept what Jesus offered.

All of this makes sense only if we acknowledge that God has fallen in love with us, madly in love. His love is without conditions, without limits. God sings of his love for us in the infinite variety of creation, in the mountains and rivers, in the flowers and the birds, in the stars, in the complexities of the human body and the human mind. Because God is in love with us, God is wildly generous to us. God lavishes gifts on us: the special blend of talents and capabilities which make each of us who we are; the love of family and friends which so enriches our human existence; wonderful surprises that come in our life, sometimes in such abundance that we don't even notice them.

Because of the love God bears us, God wants to be in our company even to the point of coming to us in human flesh. In the person of Jesus, God shares our sorrows and our frustrations, our achievements and our joys.

God takes us back when we have sinned. God brings us

together into the faith-family that is the Church. And at the end God promises us a kind of happiness that is so great that we cannot even understand it. It almost seems that God cannot help loving us. God is crazy about us.

We are called to play a part in a cosmic love story, the story of God's infinite fascination with each of us. The significance of our lives, our meaning, our worth, our value have their origin and their goal in the infinite love of the infinite God. That's the reality to which we give ourselves in faith. That's what we believe. That's why we believe.

To believe is to respond, and the only appropriate response to love is love. The only appropriate response to a love which has given us everything is to love with everything that we have, everything that we are. Our love for God is a wretched thing compared with the depth and power of God's love for us. Yet that is all that God asks of us.

We express our love for God in our acceptance of the part assigned to us in the cosmic love story. We express our love for God in the reverence and respect we show for what God has taught us, in reaching out to him in faith. The stumbling generosity we offer to our fellow human beings is an expression of our love for God.

But love also calls for explicit expression. Lovers talk to each other. We express our love for God in prayer.

Perhaps this way:

Dear God, you overwhelm us. Your wonders are so great that they stun our imaginations.

You have given us a world so beautiful that even the most eloquent of us cannot adequately express the beauty of it, so complex that even the most intelligent of us cannot fully understand even a small part of it.

- You have given each of us a unique human existence, a part to play in your story that no one else has ever played before, that no one else will ever play again. You call us to work with you in your story.

- You invite us to continue the part that you yourself played in our world in Christ Jesus. You enable us to bring his love and his service to women and men in our own little context. You invite us to worship you in union with Christ through his Church.

- Dear God, you teach us that our lives are important, not because *we* make them so but because *you* do. You are patient with us when our response to your love is flawed. You stand by us in every event of our lives and, when its end arrives, you are there, too, ready to bring us home to you forever. You promise us eternal life, eternal happiness with you.

- You have issued us an invitation, requesting the pleasure of our company here, now and forever, offering us the joy of your company in return. Your company frees us from anxiety, loneliness, failure, absurdity, discouragement.

- Dear Lord, all this is sometimes hard for us to understand. Sometimes the hustle and bustle of life make us nearsighted. We find it hard to focus on the larger picture. Sometimes what you say to us seems too good to be true. At other times, when what you ask of us seems too great for our strength, we are tempted to think that our part in your story is unplayable—or not really a part at all.

    Yet when we reflect on what you have done for us and what you have made us to be, we know that we are destined for something far greater than pain and failure.

It is hard for us to understand, Lord, not because it is too little but because it is almost too much. Perhaps the most difficult thing of all to understand, though, is simply that you really love us as much as you say you do. It doesn't make sense. We certainly don't deserve it. You certainly are not better off for it. Yet you love us anyway, wildly, measurelessly, almost madly. And in acknowledging and accepting that love lies our meaning and our salvation.

We believe, Lord, we believe.

Amen.

For Discussion

1) How do you understand that God's love is the foundation of faith?

2) In spite of our faults and failings God has fallen madly in love with us. How does God express such crazy love?

3) What part have you been given to play in God's cosmic love story?

4) What prayer might you offer to God while contemplating the meaning of life itself?